The Irrefutable Path To Power

STRATEGIES

For Building Self-esteem, Influence and Power

Tips
On how to achieve success In Leadership

Zaram N.N

Copyright © 2023 by Zaram N.N

All rights reserved. No part of this publication may be reproduced, distributed, or transmitted in any form or by any means, including photocopying, recording, or other electronic or mechanical methods, without the prior written permission of the publisher, except in the case of brief quotations embodied in critical reviews and certain other noncommercial uses permitted by copyright law. For permission requests, write to the publisher, addressed "Attention: Permissions Coordinator," at the address below.

LZR Publications and Press

176 New Umuahia Road, Aba

Abia State

Chizaramnnachi2000@gmail.com

Zaram N.N

First Edition

Disclaimer:

The information provided in this book is stated to be truthful and consistent, in that any liability, in terms of inattention or otherwise, by any usage or abuse of any policies, processes, or directions contained within is the solitary and utter responsibility of the recipient reader. Under no circumstances will any legal responsibility or blame be held against the publisher for any reparation, damages, or monetary loss due to the information herein, either directly or indirectly.

CONTENTS

Dedication

Acknowledgement

Author's note to the reader

PHASE 1 | Self Esteem

Introduction / *Page 11*

Path One / *Page 13*

PRACTICE SELF-CARE

Path two / *Page 16*

SET GOALS AND WORK TOWARDS THEM

Path Three / *Page 18*

SURROUND YOURSELF WITH POSITIVE PEOPLE

Path Four / *Page 20*

LEARN TO FORGIVE PEOPLE

Path Five / *Page 22*

PRACTICE GRATITUDE

Path Six / *Page 24*

SEEK SUPPORT

Path Seven / *Page 26*

TAKE CARE OF YOUR PHYSICAL APPEARANCE

PHASE 2 | Influence

Introduction / *Page 31*

Path Eight / *Page 33*

BUILD CREDIBILITY

Path Nine / *Page 36*

COMMUNICATE EFFECTIVELY

Path Ten / *Page 39*

LEAD BY EXAMPLE

Path Eleven / *Page 42*

FOSTER RELATIONSHIPS

Path Twelve / *Page 45*

BE AUTHENTIC

Path Thirteen / *Page 48*

BE A PROBLEM-SOLVER

Path Fourteen / *Page 51*

PRACTICE EMPATHY

PHASE 3 | Power

Introduction / *Page 57*

Path Fifteen / *Page 58*

SET GOALS AND EXPECTATIONS AND COMMUNICATE THEM CLEARLY

Path Sixteen / *Page 61*

BUILD STRONG RELATIONSHIPS

Path Seventeen / *Page 64*

STAY INFORMED

Path Eighteen / *Page 67*

BE FLEXIBLE

Path Nineteen / *Page 70*

USE YOUR POWER RESPONSIBLY

Tips On How To Achieve Success In Leadership

#1 | *Page 74*

Communicate Clearly

#2 | *Page 77*

Set Realistic Goals

#3 | *Page 80*

Delegate Tasks

#4 | *Page 83*

Provide Feedback

#5 | *Page 86*

Encourage Collaboration

#6 | *Page 89*

Support and Motivate

#7 | *Page 92*

Foster a Positive Work Environment

Conclusion | *Page 95*

Dedication

This book is dedicated to my late mother whose unending love and care nurtured me to the person I have become.

Acknowledgements

I would like to express my gratitude to the following persons for their invaluable contributions to this book.

First and foremost, I would like to thank my editor, Grace N.I, for her unwavering support and guidance throughout the writing process. Her insight and expertise were invaluable, and I'm deeply grateful for her help.

I would like to thank my family and friends for their love and encouragement during the writing process. Their support meant the world to me and I'm deeply grateful for their help.

Finally, I would like to thank all of the readers of this book. Your support and encouragement are what make this work possible, and I'm deeply grateful for your kind works and feedback.

Thank you all for your help and support. This book would not have been possible without you.

Author's note to the reader

Dear reader,

Welcome to The Path to Power: Strategies for Building Self-esteem, Influence and Power. In this book, we will explore the relationship between self-esteem and influence, and how developing strong self-esteem can help you build influence in your personal and professional life, as well as to help you learn how to manage the power that your influence will bring you.

Self-esteem is a crucial part of our overall well-being and can have a major impact on the way we view ourselves and our place in the world. It can also play a key role in our ability to influence others, as confident individuals are often better able to inspire and motivate others to take action.

In this book, we will discuss the various factors that contribute to self-esteem and how to build and maintain healthy self-esteem. We will also explore the ways in which self-esteem can be used to build influence and inspire others, and how to recognize and prevent the abuse of power.

Power is a complex and multifaceted concept that plays a significant role in our lives. It can be used for good or for ill, and it can have a profound impact on the people around us. In this book, we will delve into the various forms of power that exist and how they can be used effectively in different situations. We will also discuss the ways in which power can be abused, and how to recognize and prevent such abuse.

Whether you are seeking to boost your own self-esteem or looking to improve your ability to influence others, this book will provide you with valuable insights and strategies for achieving your goals.

Are you are a leader seeking to improve your management skills, or an individual looking to better understand the role of power in your own life, this book will provide you with valuable insights and strategies for navigating the complexities of power.

I hope that this book will serve as a useful resource for you as you seek to build confidence and inspire others in your personal and professional life.

Sincerely,

Zaram N.N.

PHASE 1

SELF-ESTEEM

Self-esteem is an important part of a healthy and happy life. It is simply the way we value ourselves

INTRODUCTION

Self-esteem is an important part of our overall well-being and can have a major impact on the way we view ourselves and our place in the world. It is the way we value and perceive ourselves, and it can influence our relationships, work, and overall happiness.

People with high self-esteem tend to have a positive view of themselves and their abilities, and are more likely to feel confident and capable. They are also more likely to have healthy relationships and to be able to cope with challenges and setbacks.

On the other hand, people with low self-esteem may have a negative view of themselves and may struggle with feelings of inadequacy and self-doubt. This can lead to problems in relationships and work, and can have a negative impact on overall well-being.

It is important to work on building and maintaining healthy self-esteem, as it can have a positive impact on our lives in many ways. This can involve learning to recognize and challenge negative thought patterns, setting achievable goals, and practicing self-care and self-compassion.

Self-esteem is an important part of a healthy and happy life. It is the way we view and value ourselves, and it can have a big impact on our relationships, work, and overall well-being. If you're looking to boost your self-esteem, here are some tips that may help:

PATH ONE

PRACTICE SELF-CARE

Take care of your physical and emotional needs by getting enough sleep, eating well, and engaging in activities that bring you joy and relaxation.

Self-care refers to the actions and activities that we take to maintain our physical, emotional, and mental well-being. It is an important part of maintaining overall health and happiness, and it can involve a wide range of activities, such as:

Eating a healthy diet:

This can help us maintain our physical health and energy levels.

Getting enough sleep:

Adequate sleep is essential for physical and mental health, and can help us feel more energized and alert.

Exercise:

Regular physical activity can help improve our physical and mental health, and can reduce stress and improve mood.

Relaxation and stress management:

Engaging in activities that help us relax and manage stress, such as meditation, yoga, or taking a warm bath, can help us feel more calm and centered.

Social connections:

Building and maintaining strong social connections can help improve our emotional well-being and provide support during difficult times.

Hobbies and leisure activities:

Engaging in activities that we enjoy, such as hobbies or leisure activities, can help improve our mood and provide a sense of purpose and accomplishment.

Self-care is an ongoing process, and it is important to make time for it in our busy lives. By prioritizing self-care, we can improve our overall well-being and feel more balanced and energized.

PATH
TWO

SET GOALS AND WORK TOWARDS THEM:

Accomplishing small tasks and achieving your goals can help boost your self-esteem and give you a sense of accomplishment.

When my niece was born, I was opportune to spend quality time with her. I literally watched her grow. When she took her first steps, I remember the excitement and joy it brought her. She wanted to take several more steps, she kept trying to run, despite falling several times.

The same is the case with everyone one of us in different aspects of our lives. When we set out to try new things, no matter how small the task maybe, we always have a little sense of accomplishment and joy in our heart when we achieve that goal. This will make us want to do more. We become a little less afraid to try new things, and before you know it, we're already doing the big stuff.

Achieving set goals can help to boost self esteem because it helps to build a sense of competence and accomplishment. When we successfully complete a task or achieve a goal, it gives us a sense of pride and satisfaction, which can contribute to feelings of self worth and confidence. Additionally, achieving goals can also help to improve our sense of agency and control over our lives, which can further contribute to increased self esteem. Finally, achieving goals can also help to build a sense of accomplishment and drive to continue striving for success, which can also have a positive impact on self esteem.

PATH
THREE

SURROUND YOURSELF WITH POSITIVE PEOPLE

Surrounding yourself with supportive and positive people can help you feel good about yourself and your choices.

Having positive relationships can have a number of benefits, including improving your mental and emotional well-being, helping you feel more supported, and making life more enjoyable.

Positive people tend to have a more optimistic outlook on life, which can be contagious. Being around positive people can help you to see things in a more positive light and can inspire you to approach challenges with a more positive attitude. Positive people also tend to be more supportive and understanding, which can help you feel more confident and motivated.

That being said, it's important to also have a balance in your relationships and to have some people in your life who challenge you and offer a different perspective. It's also important to cultivate your own positivity, rather than relying on others to lift your mood.

PATH
FOUR

LEARN TO FORGIVE YOURSELF

It's natural to make mistakes, and it's important to learn from them and move on.

Forgiving yourself can help you to let go of negative feelings, such as guilt and self-blame, and can help you to move forward and learn from your mistakes.

It's natural to feel remorse or regret when you make a mistake, but it's important to remember that everyone makes mistakes and that they are a normal part of life. Instead of dwelling on your mistakes, try to focus on what you can learn from them and how you can prevent similar mistakes in the future.

Forgiving yourself can also help you to be more compassionate towards yourself and to have more self-acceptance. It's important to treat yourself with kindness and understanding, rather than being overly critical or self-blaming.

That being said, it's also important to take responsibility for your actions and to make amends if necessary. If you have hurt someone else or caused harm, it's important to try to make things right and to learn from your mistakes.

Don't dwell on past mistakes, be kind to yourself!

PATH
FIVE

PRACTICE GRATITUDE

Focusing on the things you are grateful for can help you appreciate yourself and your accomplishments.

Gratitude involves being thankful for the good things in your life and recognizing the value of the people and things that contribute to your well-being.

Focusing on what you are grateful for can help you to see the positive aspects of your life, rather than dwelling on negative thoughts or experiences. This can help you to feel more positive about yourself and your life, which can in turn boost your self-esteem.

In addition, expressing gratitude to others can make you feel good about yourself, as it allows you to appreciate and acknowledge the contributions of others. It can also help you to build and strengthen your relationships with others, which can further contribute to your self-esteem.

That being said, it's important to remember that self-esteem is not solely based on gratitude or any one factor. It's a multifaceted concept that is influenced by a variety of factors, including your relationships, your accomplishments, and your own self-perception.

PATH
SIX

SEEK SUPPORT

It can be helpful to talk to a therapist or trusted friend or family member about your self-esteem and any issues you may be facing.

Seeking help for personal or emotional issues can be a positive step towards improving your self-esteem. It can show that you are taking responsibility for your well-being and are committed to making positive changes in your life.

Seeking help can take many forms, such as talking to a trusted friend or family member, seeking support from a mental health professional, or joining a support group. These types of resources can provide you with the support and guidance you need to work through your challenges and develop healthy coping skills.

In addition, seeking help can give you the opportunity to learn more about yourself and your strengths, and can help you to develop a greater understanding and acceptance of yourself. This can contribute to an increased sense of self-worth and self-esteem.

It's important to remember that seeking help is a sign of strength and courage, and it can be an important step towards improving your mental and emotional well-being.

PATH SEVEN

TAKE CARE OF YOUR PHYSICAL APPEARANCE

Taking care of your appearance, such as by dressing in clothes that make you feel good about yourself, can help boost your self-esteem.

Good physical appearance can be one factor that can contribute to self-esteem, but it is not the only factor and it is not the most important factor.

Self-esteem is a multifaceted concept that is influenced by a variety of factors, including your relationships, your accomplishments, your personal qualities, and your own self-perception. While physical appearance can be one aspect of your overall sense of self, it is not the only or most important aspect.

In fact, an overly strong focus on physical appearance can sometimes lead to negative consequences, such as low self-esteem, anxiety, and an unhealthy preoccupation with one's appearance. It's important to remember that everyone is unique and that there is no one "perfect" way to look.

It's important to focus on developing a healthy and positive self-image, rather than trying to achieve an unrealistic or unhealthy standard of physical appearance. This can involve learning to appreciate and accept your own unique qualities, rather than constantly comparing yourself to others.

In summary, self-esteem is an important aspect of our overall well-being, and it is worth investing time and effort into building and maintaining healthy self-esteem.

Remember, boosting your self-esteem is a process and it may take time. Be patient with yourself and try to focus on your strengths and positive qualities.

PHASE 2

INFLUENCE

Influence is not about manipulating or controlling others, but rather about inspiring and motivating them to take action.

INTRODUCTION

Influence over people refers to the ability to affect the thoughts, feelings, and behaviors of others. It can come from a variety of sources, including charisma, expertise, or a position of authority. People who are able to influence others are often seen as leaders and can be very effective at achieving their goals.

Self-esteem refers to an individual's overall evaluation of their own worth and value. It can be influenced by a variety of factors, including personal experiences, relationships, and societal expectations. People with high self-esteem generally feel confident in their abilities and are more likely to feel positive about themselves and their lives.

Influence and self-esteem are related in that people who feel confident in their abilities and value are more likely to be able to influence others. On the other hand, people with low self-esteem may struggle to assert themselves and may find it difficult to influence others. Therefore, developing and maintaining healthy self-esteem can be an important factor in one's ability to influence others.

It's important to remember that influence is not about manipulating or controlling others, but rather about inspiring and motivating them to take action.

Here are some tips for growing influence over people:

PATH EIGHT

BUILD CREDIBILITY

Establish yourself as an expert in your field or area of interest by gaining knowledge and experience, and sharing it with others.

Credibility refers to the trustworthiness and reliability of a person or organization, and it is an important factor in determining how much influence they will have. People are more likely to listen to and follow those who are seen as credible, and credibility can be a key factor in persuading others to take action.

There are several ways to build credibility, including:

Demonstrating expertise:

By gaining knowledge and skills in a particular area, you can establish yourself as an expert and increase your credibility.

Being consistent:

Consistently following through on commitments and behaving in a predictable manner can help build trust and credibility.

Being honest and transparent:

Being honest and transparent in your interactions with others can help build trust and credibility.

Seeking out opportunities to speak or write on topics in which you have expertise:

Sharing your knowledge and insights through public speaking or writing can help establish your credibility as an expert in your field.

Building relationships:

Building strong, positive relationships with others can help increase your credibility and influence.

By building credibility, you can increase your influence and become more effective at achieving your goals.

PATH NINE

COMMUNICATE EFFECTIVELY

Use clear and concise language when communicating with others, and actively listen to their perspective.

Communication is a key component of influence because it allows people to share ideas, persuade others to take action, and build relationships. Effective communication involves being able to clearly convey ideas and information, listen actively, and adapt your message to the needs and perspectives of your audience.

Some specific ways that communication can foster influence include:

Building trust:

By communicating honestly and transparently, you can build trust with others and increase your influence.

Persuading others:

Through the use of effective persuasive techniques, such as using logical arguments and appealing to emotions, you can influence others to take action.

Building relationships:

By engaging in open and honest communication with others, you can build strong, positive relationships that can increase your influence.

Sharing expertise:

By clearly communicating your knowledge and expertise, you can establish yourself as an expert and increase your influence.

Overall, effective communication is a vital component of influence, and being able to communicate effectively can help you achieve your goals and influence others.

PATH
TEN

LEAD BY EXAMPLE

Set a positive example for others to follow by demonstrating the behaviors and values that you wish to see in others.

There are several ways that you can use your lifestyle to influence others:

Lead by example:

By living a healthy, balanced, and ethical lifestyle, you can influence others to adopt similar behaviors.

Share your experiences:

Sharing your experiences and the lessons you have learned through your lifestyle can inspire and motivate others to make positive changes in their own lives.

Be a role model:

By being a positive role model and setting a good example for others to follow, you can influence their behavior and decisions.

Use social media:

By sharing your lifestyle and experiences on social media, you can reach a wide audience and influence others through your online presence.

Engage in public speaking or writing:

By sharing your experiences and the lessons you have learned through public speaking or writing, you can inspire and motivate others to make positive changes in their lives.

Overall, by living a positive and fulfilling lifestyle and sharing your experiences with others, you can influence others and inspire them to adopt similar behaviors and lifestyles.

PATH
ELEVEN

FOSTER RELATIONSHIPS

Take time to get to know people, show genuine interest in their lives, and be there for them when they need support.

Building strong relationships with others can be an important factor in personal and professional success. Here are a few tips for building strong relationships with people:

Be a good listener:

Show interest in others by actively listening to what they have to say.

Show empathy:

Try to understand and relate to others' feelings and experiences.

Be reliable and dependable:

Follow through on your commitments and be there for others when they need you.

Communicate openly and honestly:

Be open and transparent in your communication, and be honest about your thoughts and feelings.

Be respectful:

Treat others with kindness, respect, and consideration.

Be supportive:

Offer help and encouragement to others when they need it.

Be patient:

Building strong relationships takes time, and it's important to be patient and understanding.

By following these tips, you can build strong, positive relationships with others that will be beneficial for both you and the other person.

Building strong relationships with others is essential for growing influence. Take time to get to know people, show genuine interest in their lives, and be there for them when they need support.

PATH
TWELVE

BE AUTHENTIC

Be authentic and genuine in your interactions with people. People are more likely to follow someone they believe is genuine and honest.

Genuine and authentic interactions involve being genuine and authentic in your communication and relationships with others. This means being honest and transparent, being true to your values and beliefs, and being open to others' perspectives and ideas.

Genuine and authentic interactions can foster influence in several ways:

Building trust:

By being genuine and authentic in your interactions, you can build trust with others and increase your influence.

Connecting with others:

Genuine and authentic interactions allow you to connect with others on a deeper level, which can increase your influence and persuasion.

Being relatable:

Being genuine and authentic in your interactions can make you more relatable to others, which can increase your influence.

Being seen as a credible source:

By being genuine and authentic, you can establish yourself as a credible source of information and increase your influence.

Overall, genuine and authentic interactions can foster influence by building trust, connecting with others, and establishing credibility

PATH
THIRTEEN

BE A PROBLEM-SOLVER

*Look for ways to help others solve their problems
or meet their needs.*

This can help you establish yourself as a valuable resource and build influence.

Being a problem-solver can foster influence in several ways:

Demonstrating expertise:

By consistently finding solutions to problems, you can establish yourself as an expert in your field and increase your influence.

Building trust:

By consistently finding solutions to problems, you can build trust with others and increase your influence.

Being seen as a valuable resource:

By being able to solve problems, you can become a valuable resource to others and increase your influence.

Building relationships:

By working with others to solve problems, you can build strong, positive relationships that can increase your influence.

Persuading others:

By presenting solutions to problems in a clear and compelling way, you can persuade others to take action and increase your influence.

Overall, being a problem-solver can foster influence by demonstrating expertise, building trust, being seen as a valuable resource, building relationships, and persuading others.

PATH FOURTEEN

PRACTICE EMPATHY

Showing understanding and compassion for others can help you build strong relationships and increase your influence.

Practicing empathy can foster influence in several ways:

Building trust:

By showing empathy and understanding towards others, you can build trust and increase your influence.

Connecting with others:

By showing empathy and understanding, you can connect with others on a deeper level and increase your influence.

Persuading others:

By understanding and relating to others' feelings and perspectives, you can more effectively persuade them to take action and increase your influence.

Building relationships:

By showing empathy and understanding towards others, you can build strong, positive relationships that can increase your influence.

Being seen as a credible source:

By showing empathy and understanding, you can establish yourself as a credible and reliable source of information and increase your influence.

Overall, practicing empathy can foster influence by building trust, connecting with others, persuading others, building relationships, and being seen as a credible source.

Growing influence is an ongoing process that requires consistent effort and a focus on building one's skill and relationships. It is important to use influence responsibly and with consideration for the impact on others.

Remember, growing influence is not about trying to control others, but rather about inspiring and motivating them to take positive actions!

PHASE

3

POWER

The irrefutable Path to Power

Power is the ability to influence others, to achieve goals, and to shape the world around us.

INTRODUCTION

Power is a complex and often misunderstood concept, but it is an important force in our personal and professional lives. It can be defined as the ability to influence others, to achieve goals, and to shape the world around us.

Power can come from a variety of sources, including charisma, expertise, or a position of authority. It can be used for good or for ill, and how we use our power can have a significant impact on the world around us.

Power can come from a variety of sources including charisma, expertise, or a position of authority. It can be used for good or for ill, and how we use our power can have a significant impact on the world around us.

The concept of power is multifaceted and can involve the ability to influence others, to make decisions and take action, to control resources and access to opportunities, and to shape the beliefs and behaviors of others.

Maintaining power can be challenging, especially if you are in a leadership role.

Understanding the concept of power and how it works is important for the effective leadership, personal development and social change.

Here are some tips for maintaining power:

PATH
FIFTEEN

**SET GOALS AND EXPECTATIONS AND
COMMUNICATE THEM CLEARLY**

*Clearly communicating your goals and expectations
can help you stay focused and maintain control
over your actions and decisions.*

Setting goals and expectations can foster power over people in several ways:

Establishing authority:

By setting clear goals and expectations, you can establish yourself as an authority figure and increase your power and influence.

Providing direction:

By setting clear goals and expectations, you can provide direction and guidance to others, which can increase your power and influence.

Persuading others:

By setting clear goals and expectations and explaining the reasoning behind them, you can persuade others to follow your lead and increase your power and influence.

Creating accountability:

By setting clear goals and expectations and holding others accountable for meeting them, you can increase your power and influence.

Overall, setting goals and expectations can foster power over people by establishing authority, providing direction, persuading others, and creating accountability.

However, it is important to use this power responsibly and consider the impact it may have on others.

PATH
SIXTEEN

BUILD STRONG RELATIONSHIPS

Building strong relationships with others can help you maintain power by establishing trust and respect.

Strong relationships are built on trust, mutual respect, and a shared sense of purpose, and they can provide a foundation for maintaining power and influence.

Some specific ways that building strong relationships can help to maintain power include;

Building a network of support:

By building a strong network of supportive relationships, you can increase your power and influence through the collective strength of those connections.

Establishing credibility:

By building strong relationships and consistently following through on your commitments, you can establish yourself as a credible and reliable source of information and increase your power.

Maintaining influence:

By building strong relationships, you can maintain influence by staying connected and engaged with others.

Overall, building strong relationships can help to maintain power by building a network of support, establishing credibility, and maintaining influence.

It is important to remember, however, that power and influence should be used responsibly and with consideration for the impact on others.

PATH
SEVENTEEN

STAY INFORMED

Staying informed about current events and trends in your field or industry can help you maintain power by keeping you up-to-date and relevant.

Staying informed involves keeping up-to-date on current events and developments in your field or area of expertise, and it can be an important factor in maintaining power and influence.

Staying informed can help to maintain power in several ways:

Demonstrating expertise:

By staying informed and up-to-date on current events and developments in your field, you can demonstrate your expertise and increase your power and influence.

Building credibility:

By staying informed, you can establish yourself as a credible and reliable source of information and increase your power and influence.

Maintaining influence:

By staying informed, you can maintain your influence by staying engaged and connected with others.

Being able to adapt and respond:

By staying informed, you can be better prepared to adapt to changing circumstances and respond effectively, which can increase your power and influence.

Overall, staying informed can help to maintain power by demonstrating expertise, building credibility, maintaining influence, and being able to adapt and respond to changing circumstances.

It is important to remember, however, that power and influence should be used responsibly and with consideration for the impact on others.

PATH
EIGHTEEN

BE FLEXIBLE

Being open to new ideas and approaches can help you maintain power by showing that you are adaptable and open to change.

Flexibility refers to the ability to adapt and respond to changing circumstances, and it can be an important factor in maintaining power and influence.

Some specific ways that being flexible can help to maintain power include:

Demonstrating adaptability:

By being flexible and able to adapt to changing circumstances, you can demonstrate your ability to adapt and increase your power and influence.

Building credibility:

By being flexible and able to respond effectively to changing circumstances, you can establish yourself as a credible and reliable source of information and increase your power and influence.

Maintaining influence:

By being flexible and able to adapt to changing circumstances, you can maintain your influence by staying engaged and connected with others.

Being able to respond to new challenges:

By being flexible, you can be better prepared to respond to new challenges and opportunities, which can increase your power and influence.

Overall, being flexible can help to maintain power by demonstrating adaptability, building credibility, maintaining influence, and being able to respond to new challenges.

It is important to remember, however, that power and influence should be used responsibly and with consideration for the impact on others.

PATH NINETEEN

USE YOUR POWER RESPONSIBLY

Remember that with power comes responsibility. Use your power wisely and ethically, and be mindful of the impact your actions have on others.

Power can be used responsibly in several ways:

Use power for the greater good:
Use your power and influence to make positive changes in the world and to help others.

Use power ethically:
Use your power and influence in an ethical and moral manner, taking into consideration the impact on others.

Use power to empower others:
Use your power and influence to help empower others and give them the tools and resources they need to succeed.

Use power to build strong relationships:
Use your power and influence to build strong, positive relationships with others.

By using power responsibly in these ways, you can maintain your power and influence over time.

Additionally, by using your power to make a positive impact in the world and to help others, you can increase your credibility and trustworthiness, which can further enhance your power and influence.

It is important to remember, however, that power and influence should be used with consideration for the impact on others, and that it is important to balance the use of power with ethical considerations.

Maintaining power requires a combination of strong leadership skills and the ability to adapt to changing circumstances.

By focusing on building strong relationships, staying informed, and being flexible and responsible, you can effectively maintain power in your personal and professional life.

Tips on how to achieve Success in Leadership

Managing people effectively is an important skill, especially if you have power over them in a leadership or managerial role.

Here are some tips for managing people effectively:

#1

COMMUNICATE CLEARLY

Clearly communicating your expectations and goals can help ensure that everyone is on the same page and working towards the same objectives.

Effective communication is an important skill for leaders to manage people. Communication involves the exchange of information, ideas, and thoughts through speaking, writing, or other means of expression, and it is a vital component of effective leadership.

Effective communication can help leaders to manage people in several ways:

Setting expectations:

By clearly communicating expectations and goals to team members, leaders can help to ensure that everyone is working towards the same objectives.

Providing direction:

By clearly communicating their vision and plans for the future, leaders can provide direction and guidance to their team.

Building trust:

By being open and transparent in their communication, leaders can build trust with their team and increase their effectiveness as leaders.

Resolving conflicts:

By effectively communicating and addressing conflicts as they arise, leaders can help to prevent misunderstandings and maintain a positive team environment.

Overall, effective communication is an important skill for leaders to manage people and can help to set expectations, provide direction, build trust, and resolve conflicts.

#2

SET REALISTIC GOALS

Setting realistic goals can help ensure that everyone is working towards something achievable and that their efforts are not wasted.

Setting goals is an important part of effective leadership, as it helps to provide direction and focus to team members and helps to ensure that everyone is working towards the same objectives.

Setting realistic goals can help leaders to manage people in several ways:

Providing clarity:

By setting clear, realistic goals, leaders can help to provide clarity and focus to their team.

Building trust:

By setting realistic goals and following through on them, leaders can build trust with their team and increase their effectiveness as leaders.

Motivating team members:

By setting challenging but achievable goals, leaders can motivate their team to work towards success.

Managing resources:

By setting realistic goals, leaders can better manage their team's resources and ensure that they are being used effectively.

Overall, setting realistic goals can help leaders to manage people by providing clarity, building trust, motivating team members, and managing resources.

It is important to remember, however, that goals should be challenging but achievable, and that they should be adjusted as needed to reflect changing circumstances.

#3

DELEGATE TASKS

Delegating tasks to others can help you manage your workload more effectively and allow others to develop new skills and take on more responsibility.

Delegating tasks involves assigning specific responsibilities to team members and empowering them to take ownership of their work.

Delegating tasks can help leaders to manage people in several ways:

Building team skills:

By delegating tasks, leaders can give team members the opportunity to learn new skills and develop their expertise.

Improving efficiency:

By delegating tasks to the most appropriate team members, leaders can improve efficiency and productivity.

Promoting teamwork:

By delegating tasks and encouraging collaboration, leaders can foster teamwork and a sense of shared responsibility.

Building trust:

By delegating tasks and empowering team members to take ownership of their work, leaders can build trust and increase their effectiveness as leaders.

Overall, delegating tasks can help leaders to manage people by building team skills, improving efficiency, promoting teamwork, and building trust.

It is important to remember, however, that delegation should be done in a way that is fair and appropriate to the skills and experience of team members, and that a leader should provide guidance and support as needed.

#4

PROVIDE FEEDBACK

Giving timely and constructive feedback can help people understand how they are doing and where they can improve.

Providing feedback is an important part of effective leadership, as it helps to communicate expectations, provide guidance, and support team members in their development.

Providing feedback can help leaders to manage people in several ways:

Improving performance:

By providing clear and constructive feedback, leaders can help team members understand what they are doing well and areas where they can improve, which can help to improve performance.

Building trust:

By providing regular and honest feedback, leaders can build trust with their team and increase their effectiveness as leaders.

Motivating team members:

By providing positive feedback and recognizing achievements, leaders can motivate team members to continue working towards success.

Providing support:

By providing feedback and guidance, leaders can support team members in their development and help them to achieve their goals.

Overall, providing feedback is an important way for leaders to manage people and can help to improve performance, build trust, motivate team members, and provide support.

It is important to remember, however, that feedback should be delivered in a constructive and respectful manner, and that it should be tailored to the individual needs and goals of team members.

#5

ENCOURAGE COLLABORATION

Encouraging collaboration and teamwork can help people feel more invested in their work and can lead to better outcomes.

Encouraging collaboration is an important part of effective leadership, as it helps to foster teamwork, build strong relationships, and encourage the sharing of ideas and knowledge.

Encouraging collaboration can help leaders to manage people in several ways:

Improving efficiency:

By encouraging collaboration and the sharing of ideas, leaders can improve efficiency and productivity.

Building teamwork:

By encouraging collaboration and teamwork, leaders can foster a positive team environment and a sense of shared responsibility.

Building trust:

By encouraging collaboration and the sharing of ideas, leaders can build trust with their team and increase their effectiveness as leaders.

Promoting creativity:

By encouraging collaboration and the sharing of ideas, leaders can promote creativity and encourage team members to think outside the box.

Overall, encouraging collaboration is an important way for leaders to manage people and can help to improve efficiency, build teamwork, build trust, and promote creativity.

It is important to remember, however, that collaboration should be encouraged in a way that is respectful and considerate of the needs and goals of team members.

#6

SUPPORT AND MOTIVATE

Supporting and motivating your team can help them feel valued and motivated to do their best work.

Keeping people motivated is an important part of effective leadership, as it helps to foster a positive team environment and encourage team members to work towards success.

Keeping people motivated can help leaders to manage people in several ways:

Improving performance:

By keeping team members motivated, leaders can help to improve performance and productivity.

Building teamwork:

By keeping team members motivated, leaders can foster a positive team environment and a sense of shared responsibility.

Building trust:

By keeping team members motivated and recognizing their achievements, leaders can build trust with their team and increase their effectiveness as leaders.

Promoting commitment:

By keeping team members motivated and engaged, leaders can promote commitment and encourage team members to stay with the organization.

Overall, keeping people motivated is an important way for leaders to manage people and can help to improve performance, build teamwork, build trust, and promote commitment.

It is important to remember, however, that motivation should be tailored to the individual needs and goals of team members, and that it is important to find a balance between challenge and support.

#7

FOSTER A POSITIVE WORK ENVIRONMENT

Creating a positive work environment where people feel respected and valued can help foster a sense of teamwork and collaboration, and can lead to better outcomes.

There are several ways you can create a positive work environment in your workplace as a leader:

Communicate clearly and openly:

Communicate clearly and openly with your team to ensure that everyone is on the same page and has a clear understanding of expectations and goals.

Encourage collaboration and teamwork:

Encourage collaboration and teamwork by promoting the sharing of ideas and knowledge and by fostering a sense of shared responsibility.

Recognize and reward achievement:

Recognize and reward achievement to motivate team members and show appreciation for their hard work.

Support professional development:

Support professional development by providing opportunities for learning and growth and by encouraging team members to pursue their goals.

Foster a culture of respect and inclusion:

Foster a culture of respect and inclusion by promoting diversity and inclusivity and by creating a safe and welcoming environment for all team members.

By implementing these strategies, you can create a positive work environment that is conducive to productivity, teamwork, and professional development.

It is important to remember, however, that creating a positive work environment is an ongoing process and requires consistent effort and commitment.

Effective management requires a combination of clear communication, goal setting, delegation, feedback, collaboration, support, and motivation. By focusing on these areas, you can effectively manage people and achieve your goals.

CONCLUSION

In conclusion, self-esteem, influence, and power are all complex and interrelated concepts that play a significant role in our personal and professional lives. Self-esteem is the foundation upon which we build our sense of worth and value, and it plays a crucial role in our ability to influence and exert power. Influence is the ability to shape the thoughts, feelings, and actions of others, and it can come from a variety of sources, including charisma, expertise, or a position of authority. Power is the ability to achieve goals and shape the world around us, and it can be used for good or for ill.

In order to increase our self-esteem, influence, and power, it is important to focus on building our skills, knowledge, and relationships. This can involve setting goals and expectations, staying informed and up-to-date, building credibility and trust, and practicing empathy and problem-solving. It is also important to use our self-esteem, influence, and power responsibly, with consideration for the impact on others and a focus on making a positive difference in the world.

Ultimately, self-esteem, influence, and power are powerful forces that can shape our lives and the world around us. By understanding these concepts and working to develop them, we can increase our ability to achieve our goals and make a positive impact on the world.

The irrefutable Path to PowerPage 97

www.ingramcontent.com/pod-product-compliance
Lightning Source LLC
Chambersburg PA
CBHW050245220526
45465CB00002B/561